Carry Us To The Next Well

An Anthology of Poetry

Cover photograph by Stephen Hoppe
Monument Valley, Navajo Nation

Cover design by Shay Culligan

ISBN: 978-1-954353-43-5

Kelsay Books
502 South 1040 East, A-119
American Fork, Utah 84003
Kelsaybooks.com

Dedication

We dedicate this book to our talented and generous friend, **Sandra Lynn Becker**, an original member of the Kitchen Table Poets, a poetry workshop and critique group that began gathering at Marie Kane's kitchen table in August 2009.

All of the poets in *Carry Us to the Next Well* are active members of Kitchen Table. Sandy took her participation in our critique group seriously, often carrying poems home to give further feedback. We see her insightful and revelatory commentary in this book's poems, many of which she helped to edit. We loved her for this significant poetic support, and for her intense interest in people—apparent to anyone who met her.

Sandy deeply appreciated the poets of Bucks and Montgomery Counties (PA) who offered her constant opportunity to hone her art.

She felt special gratitude to Dr. Christopher Bursk of Bucks County Community College for his steadfast mentoring, generous and valued feedback, spirit and friendship, and superlative poetry. She believed he modeled vulnerability and authenticity in all of his interactions with poets. Most importantly, he kept her striving to be a better poet; she could not imagine herself as a poet without his influence.

The following is Sandy's wish for her readers, and our wish for you:

I hope my readers take away a sense of connection from my poems— that my poems act as a bridge to one another. I hope that the reader feels a sense of beauty, and just as importantly, a sense of the mystery behind the creation of that beauty, that they feel a shared experience of creating that beauty—and, a sense of awe. And, the sense of wanting more.

Marie Kane
Wendy Fulton Steginsky

Acknowledgments

Our gratitude to the editors of the following publications where these poems first appeared, some in slightly different form or title:

Becker, Sandra. "Caravanserai." *Imperfect Matter.* WordTech Editions, 2013, p. 59.

Becker, Sandra. "Praise the Body." *Imperfect Matter.* WordTech Editions, 2013, p. 29.

Falk, Katherine Hahn. "Her Continuing Metamorphosis." *U.S. 1 Worksheets* Volume 60, 2015: 118. Print.

Falk, Katherine Hahn. "Hungry Ghosts." *U.S. 1 Worksheets* Volume 64, 2019: 107. Print.

Falk, Katherine Hahn. "Questions That Concern Me." *U.S. 1 Worksheets* Volume 62, 2017: 125. Print.

Fanok, Lynn. "Cliff Swallows." Bread and Fumes, Kelsay Books, 2021, p. 26.

Fanok, Lynn. "A Visit to the Country." Bread and Fumes, Kelsay Books, 2021, p. 20.

Fanok, Lynn. "Wood and Bone." Bread and Fumes, Kelsay Books, 2021, p. 28.

Jerome, Mary Jo LoBello. "A Black Stone." *Schuylkill Valley Journal* Spring 2019: 120. Print.

Jerome, Mary Jo LoBello. "Tokyo Underground Prayer." *River Heron Review* August 2018. Online.

Kane, Marie. "Balanced Enough." *Pentimento* Fall 2013: 35. Print.

Kane, Marie. "Beauty, You Drive a Hard Bargain." *Something On Our Minds: An Anthology to Benefit the Accelerated Cure Project for M.S., Vol. III.* Eds.: Laura Kolaczkowski, et al. We Write for The Fight, 2015, p. 116.

Kane, Marie. "Third-Quarter Moon." *Schuylkill Valley Journal* Spring 2019: 93. Print.

Kumar, Lavinia. "Birds in the Mist." *Mobius* Volume XXX, 2012: 35. Print.

Kumar, Lavinia. "Orphan Train." *Ascent Aspiration* 27 July 2018. Online.

Kumar, Lavinia. "A Slave Catches God's Eye." *Orbis* Spring 2017: 43. Print.

McBride, Bernadette. "After 'Only until this cigarette is ended.' " *Mezzo Cammin* Summer 2018. Online.

McBride, Bernadette. "And the Cheese Stands Alone." *Schuylkill Valley Journal* Spring 2013: 35. Print.

McBride, Bernadette. "Counter." *Postcard Poems and Prose Magazine* Winter 2018. Online.

McKee, Christine Caruso. "When One of Us Is No Longer." *On Shady Lane,* WordTech Editions, 2015, p. 62.

Miller, Mary Richardson. "Madeline Albright's Cleavage." *Love Over 60: An Anthology of Women's Poems*, eds.: Robin Chapman, Jeri McCormick, Mayapple Press, 2010, p. 67.

Miller, Mary Richardson. "Urban Remedies." *U.S. 1 Worksheets* Volume 65, 2020. Print.

Nolan, Steve. "Naming Fireflies." *River Heron Review* February 2020. Online.

Steginsky, Wendy Fulton. "Twilight's Small Gestures." *River Heron Review* August 2019. Online.

Steginsky, Wendy Fulton. "Ursula." *Let This Be Enough,* Kelsay Books, 2016, p. 35.

Steginsky, Wendy Fulton. "Ursula Comes into Her Own & How." *When River's Mouth Meets Ocean,* Kelsay Books, 2019, p. 42.

Wrzesniewski, Connie. "Full Moon on a November Night in the Woods of Hickory Run." *Hawk and Whippoorwill* Summer 2019: 6. Print and online.

Foreword

"Slapped into the loud insistent world / a wailing body / you find your voice," begins "Praise the Body," the very first poem of *Carry Us to the Next Well*, a gathering of work by the Kitchen Table Poets. That the book ambushes us right away with Sandra Becker's sudden past participle packed with implications reminds us that we are often *startled* into poetry, finding ourselves immersed in a world that is loud and often relentlessly insistent. And finding our voices is often a matter of survival. This is true of each of the poets within this collection; each in her or his own way has responded to the world's often oppressive demands with poetry's always liberating demands: that call to a new kind of justice possible only from language.

In May 1991 *The Atlantic* published what proved to be a controversial commentary on the state of poetry in America. The title of Dana Gioia's essay was "Can Poetry Matter?" and its subtitle argued that "Poetry has vanished as a cultural force in America. If poets venture outside their confined world, they can work to make it essential once more." As *Carry Us to the Next Well* makes clear, page by page, poetry is very much a "cultural force," in that it has the power still to transform lives. This power is accessible to and has an impact on all aspects of the culture, whether it be exploring Madeline Albright's cleavage or Musica Universalis, the snake in the garden or an orphan train, cliff swallows or hungry ghosts, living with MS or after Afghanistan.

To ask poets to "venture outside their confined world," as Gioia does, is to ignore Emily Dickinson's adventures or Stevie Smith's or Keats's and, in fact, to overlook the paradox at the heart of poetry: its confined space is the source of our freedom. Its compression offers so much room for intense investigation. It sets boundaries it immediately tests. At different points in *Carry Us to the Next Well*, we are on the Tokyo Underground or on the topmost bluff overlooking the Missouri or in Rwanda or storming across the Ben Franklin Bridge and then we are driving to the moon. We get to know the kick-ass-chick Ursula; a cat with the moniker Miss Simone de Beauvoir; a slave sewing a hat to catch God's eye; and, sitting on a tractor, a young girl with Down syndrome and named for a Bible queen—"She's shy of strangers but / loves heavy equipment." We even encounter Leonardo da Vinci, boarding a Virgin America flight. We feast on Bapcia's rhubarb pie, rich Gorgonzola, Uncle Joe's chili sauce, as well as the "last blooms of Annabelle hydrangea," the "scarlet bell of a newly bloomed Eastern Columbine," and the "linguistics of silver leaf." But we also witness a knife-wielding father, the abduction of a child, the death of a friend by her own hand, the picnic for another relative off to war.

"The problem of suffering in the world / frequently keeps me from joy," writes one of the poets—and he should know, given his tour of duty in Afghanistan and his battle with bone cancer. But his poem "I Can't Seem to Meditate Any Longer" ends in an embrace of laughter—"the one sound you can still believe / is an answer to your prayers." This is a book of elegy but also of awe. "I don't believe October. / Those trees up the hill could not have turned / such color overnight," writes one poet, and another invokes that "sudden hitch of breath / at the expanse of sea" at her feet.

Carry Us to the Next Well is curated with an intelligence that makes this more than a collection of poems; it is a crafted testimony to the hard bargains that beauty demands of every poet and every poem, every "dream covered with grit."

The book unfolds in four sections, inviting us first to open ourselves to the metaphysical questions rooted in our daily experience; those questions do not just concern us, they get us a little dizzy, as Katherine Falk acknowledges. "Sometimes I think a thousand / thoughts at once. I have to stand still for this." That's what a poem does: it stands still and, in its confined world, offers us a focused and thus liberated space and time to explore. Section II locates us in place—"Pot by pot I plant herbs, / a language learned from my mother" and family. Section III locates us in time—"summer of the blue sarong," "twilight's small gestures," and "third-quarter moon." Section IV embraces the resonant particulars of the world: a lopsided black stone "water worn with pleasing heft," wooden Polish icon of Mary next to "small carved birds," the "timbre of plate on table" and that "harvesting," that "celebratory feasting" that comes, as Phyllis Purscell posits:

> When all the promises you have made
> to yourself and others have been kept
>
> or broken, and you can acknowledge
> that everything will be all right
>
> Or it won't.

—that acceptance that sometimes seems possible only in poetry. Poetry is perhaps the most "forgiving" of the arts; the very fact that lines stop and pause, break and then gather their resolve to continue is one of the loveliest admissions of fallibility and faith I know.

This book presents the work of the Kitchen Table Poets, one of those communities throughout the world that, in their craft and commitment, testify to the truth that poetry can and does matter. In her poem. "At the Kitchen Table," Monica Flint includes us in her encounter with "The Buddha, Jesus, Muhammad / Praise Be Upon Him, and Moses," all of them "instantly recognizable." And real? "As real as the oracles. / As real as eggs is eggs!"

Remarkable things can happen at a kitchen table. This book is proof of that fact. It is thus proof that poets flourish when they find a community that both challenges and supports; that holds each poem to the fire and encourages each poet to be faithful to the poem she or he is forging in that fire, "in sync with the universe" yet "restless" at the same time.

What happens at a kitchen table can, as Christine McKee suggests, "someday hold an / extraordinarily / exquisite / beauty."

"We made a song / we couldn't sing. / You had your nerve / I had mine" writes Elizabeth Rivers in "Mouth Painted Card," a poem "for Sandy," and in this lyric makes a song, as so many brave poets have done before, out of what seems to defy song.

What is perhaps most to be admired in *Carry Us to the Next Well* is the nerve of these poets. And of these poems! Lynda Gene Rymond in her "How Should We Then Pray" concludes "maybe…I'll just sing out / every now and again." Ah, the nerve of her. The nerve of poetry itself.

"Night is falling" and we need someone to lead us home.

The spirit of Sandra Becker presides over *Carry Us to the Next Well*. Her lyric poems begin and conclude the book and provide the epigraphs for each section. This book honors her memory by asserting just how emphatically poetry does matter. It takes its title from her poem "Caravanserai," an allegory of a pilgrimage across a difficult landscape, following the call of an invisible flute. This world can be a desert that seems often impossible to traverse, but poetry can carry us to the next well. All of us. It's that obliging, that sure-footed.

~ Christopher Bursk

Contents

III

IV

Praise the Body

Sandra Becker

Slapped into the loud insistent world,
a wailing body,
you find your voice—
wheeze, croupy cough,
inarticulate bark.

In time, you learn
to douse and unearth
the precise words
you come to need,
hide them in a chest
return to them
on days the impertinent sun
refuses to show its face

and the moon, well,
the moon, hardly a sliver
of consolation
with its idiot promises,
high tide that pulls you in
and dashes you against
the unyielding rocks. No matter,

you lift each syllable from its dark
bed, place it
on your tongue, allow it
to speak to you
in a half-forgotten language.

I

"You've been guided to precisely this place at precisely this time."

~ Sandra Becker, "Signs of God," *Dread Islands*

Ursula

Wendy Fulton Steginsky

Inside dwells a kick-ass chick named Ursula
who wears black leather punched up
with brass buttons, knee-high, silver-studded boots
and a sultry smile wrapped around a smoldering Marlboro.

Ursula's sworn to keep me safe—her finely tuned
bullshit detector knows I hate it when someone says
one thing and does another. Always 15 and ½ she leans
into a cement wall, one foot cocked against it.

But Ursula can't see beyond that wall. Like a blind person
she needs to feel her way to an opening
or a spot where the wall loses resistance.
Sometimes she'll sense it soften and undulate

as a moonlight's rippling ribbon that allows her
to spy an orchard of charred apple trees
that sift to ash when touched,
a pile of gray memories and chewed bits of bone,

worn down to something she can inhale.
In the distance, a mansion with many rooms,
encircled by sprawling wildflowers becomes
a dream covered with grit, a vision drunk with time.

Ursula says as long as God's in the sky and she's in charge,
I can die at night, reinvent myself wrapped in peach silk
and silvering birch leaves for all she cares. Just as long as I nod
from the mountaintop, leave her the outlying zones.

Madeline Albright's Cleavage   *Mary Richardson Miller*

I race to hear Madeline Albright speak at the Miami
Book Fair, ambassador, peacemaker, my hero,
a woman smart enough to know the original Hero
was a woman, her name purloined by envious Greek males.
In high hopes I reach the auditorium only to find it filled.
Dejected, I descend the escalator just as
Madame Secretary ascends en route to the podium,
dressed in power suit, signature pin, and on display
her most magnificent cleavage glowing in Miami heat.
Then she disappears. But so does distress when I realize
I'm here to be happy, for happiness is city blocks
filled with books. Scheduled next is a reading
by powerful, prolific Joyce Carol Oates who tells
eager writers like me not to take ourselves
so seriously, that even if we heave our guts, it's
only a book. Next I sprint to a corner gallery to hear
passionate poets recite poems from anthologies
written by women over sixty. And I pause
to reflect: on cleavage. I know how old my hero is.
My age. I have only to look. What some call mature,
I call ripe. What some call sex, I call desire.
Happiness is to be on fire. I learned that from books.

Beauty, You Drive a Hard Bargain   *Marie Kane*

Oh!—Beauty! You drive a hard bargain. You'll repair
        my shrinking good looks and dysfunctional body,
and I'll give you carte blanche with most of the lavish
        wardrobe and jewelry that my crippled body no longer
wears—and then, I'll write Odes singing your magnificence!

You relish wearing my high-heeled shoes—their rhinestones
        announce your presence with every step.
When removed at night, they swing from your exquisitely
        manicured red nails as you place them on the closet
shoe-shelf. You treasure my dresses—slits on sheer crepe,
        short, swingy skirts, blushing, strapless beauties.
Your wondrous bosom fills my fashionable cashmere
        sweaters and when adored, you bashfully lower
your Victoria's Secret eyes.

But you went too far, dear Beauty. Weren't you twirling
        in my heels on *Dancing with the Stars*, caressing
my elegant sable wrap that you stole? When I couldn't
        find it on my closet's top shelf where I hide
precious things, I didn't want to suspect you. We had
        made our bargain: I gave you stylish clothes
and flattering Odes, while you guaranteed that my
        disability would vanish and my smile would stay.

But Beauty—you traitorous vixen! I should have known
        that your hesitancy when shaking hands foretold
betrayal. I have not been the same since you, Beauty,
        with all your glitz and glamor, posed demurely
in the back seat, my sapphire and diamond necklace
        flashing at the nape of your soft neck—while the Burden
of Disability sat up front with me and madly drove the car.

21

How Should We Then Pray?

Lynda Gene Rymond

Maura drove the tractor over—
there must have been a reason,
for she never wastes time or anything else.
Also her youngest came,
who is named for a Bible queen
and has Down syndrome.

She is shy of strangers but
loves heavy equipment.
I see her at a distance,
on a lap, helping to steer
tractor, mower, backhoe—
tiny blonde head sandwiched between
enormous pink ear protectors.

Maura cut the motor
and I approached.
The little one slid down, peeled off her headphones,
gave me a wide berth
and disappeared into the berry patch
as quickly and completely
as a shiny baby snake.

Her voice piped
I'm here!
I'm here!
and again
I'm here!

We can't keep her from running off to the woods,
Maura said. *(I'm here!)*
but she's willing to let us know where she is.
(I'm here!)

Later, I thought how prayers get to be lists
and how boring that must get
for an all-knowing God
So maybe instead, I'll just sing out

every now and again
to say:

(I'm here!)
I'm in the woods but unafraid

(I'm here!)
or maybe a little afraid

(I'm here!)
or that night is falling
and I need someone to lead me home.

A Slave Catching God's Eye

Lavinia Kumar

My lord, see my hat, hear my prayers.
I have paid for an extra feather
that this fine head cover
will be closer to you. My head
is high, and my back straight
that it might reach you. Please
take it if you see fit. Or the beads,
the blue and white ones ready
for your sky, dear lord.

Each day I watch for clouds, rain,
that my body will cool, and pray
you'll see my hair is gathered
into a simple wrap, though my arms
are bare. But so tired. Each night
I dream. Each eve I sew a hat
to surely catch your eye on Sunday—
to save us from our terrible days,
to let us live in freedom.

My lord, my head is wrapped
as you decree. My man calls each hat
a crown, and it is my true self, if alone
for this one day. I am proud to stand tall,
that in church I am respected woman.
But my hat is a call to you, a call to see
all of us plain souls who are in need.
Oh, my lord, see my hat,
please, now, hear my prayer.

Questions That Concern Me

Katherine Hahn Falk

Let's say it's true
what Buddha shared
about the endless succession of lives.

How many cells are in a body?
Is that an endless succession
of growing, multiplying,

rejuvenating that stops
only with death
as the endless succession of lives

stops only with enlightenment?
It's said that everyone we've ever looked
in the eye, we've met in another life.

It becomes mathematics,
it becomes drama. It becomes
the flow of music. When I first learned

about reincarnation, Rimbaud's *Season In Hell*
and *Illuminations* spoke my thoughts
so I figured I may have been him for one life.

What about family; that we choose our family
by what we can teach each other, that we repeat lives
with the same family members but switch places?

Was I a Bedouin son and you
the mother, or a dolphin
in your pod; the bull, cow or calf?

Are our lives limited to this planet,
this galaxy? Sometimes I think a thousand
thoughts at once. I have to stand still for this.

Naming Fireflies

Steve Nolan

They appear and disappear like a meteor shower—
if meteors could be resurrected to new life
after burning out.
                          We spread our blanket,
unpack a picnic lunch as the sun sets
on Tanglewood's evening concert series.
Tonight: J.S. Bach, who, many say,
could hear the music of spheres,
inspiring concertos, consecrating mass.
I don't know how many patrons share
Bach's faith, but all see these pulsations
of light in the darkening air. Too dark
now to see their bodies, but with great
concentration it is possible to follow
the flight path of a single lightning bug.
I make a game of this, foiled when
they cross paths with another.
                          I'm not cruel
but I remember trapping them in jars,
martyring them to possess their light, showing
off for other kids. We once smeared
their abdomens as eye shadow on Halloween,
that night that ushers in darkness
for all souls.
                          We feel the envelope
of night descend. Bach suddenly joins
the light parade and I question if I've drunk
too much wine because I swear they're blinking
in sync with the Musica Universalis—
celestial bodies: sun, moon, planets,
lightning bugs in orbit.

                    My wife takes
my hand. She is moved by the music.
I wonder if she is thinking of Yemen or Syria,
the peace and reconciliation work
she does in Rwanda. If she squeezes hard
I know she will make me cry. There are
many light workers in the world, so much
darkness I am staring into—straining not
to lose sight of Jesus, Buddha, Gandhi—
it is the wine!
                    I am naming fireflies.

Snake in the Garden

Lynda Gene Rynond

I dug potatoes,
or tried to,
when the garter snake—
seven inches long,
fierce as a rattler—
roiled and snapped,
hating me,
my boots, my shovel.

Ease up, I said.
I planted these potatoes
back in spring,
need them for my dinner
and you've only been alive
a few days.

I have lived here my whole life
and it is all mine.
Snake came at me again,
mouth smaller than a thimble.

So I took my shovel
way down the row,
dug moist fingerlings
thought about equivalencies,
also possession,
land deeds,
the courage
of those just born.

Dear Mr. Darwin

Monica Borrin Flint

The ruby-throated hummingbird, recently returned
from Mexico, halts—abrupt, suspended,
seemingly motionless
before the scarlet bell of a newly bloomed

Eastern Columbine; its nectar cached
inside long spurs, too deep for a bee's reach,
but calibration-perfect for a hummer's slender bill
and extended tongue. While the hovering

bird minutely adjusts position
to sip the sugary drink, the flower's
pollen, a dusting on tiny protruding stamens
can't but brush against the hummingbird's head.

That caressing, repeated as the bird feasts
from columbine to columbine, spreads
the gold-dust from male to female, and thus
the avian go-between unwittingly sparks seed.

No accident, though, the bird's return to Philadelphia
just as the Aquilegias bloom,
no lucky chance the depth of the spurs,
the length of the bill and tongue.

Becoming

Elizabeth Rivers

New budding
branch
rises and falls,
sighs
in the rain.

When I am
leaf and air
I too
will Monet
your window.

The Blue Sky

for Sandy

The bluest of blue skies, its wide expanse
a broad umbrella from east to west,
north to south and every space in-between.
Bluer than the eye of a white-furred huskie,
keener than the blue
in Bellini's *Ecstasy of St. Francis.*

Accented by the unexpected snow fall,
barely enough to close schools though it does,
children in plaid jackets and black boots
with their redder-than-red saucer sleds,
up the hill and down—their squeals echo
above the naked tree limbs crusted in ice.

Later, the sun begins to warm the snow
and the toes and the noses of the sledders,
packed-down paths become slippery,
shiny slices of light that divide the day.
Mothers call their children home
for hot chocolate and graham crackers.

Ribbons of deep pink and gold highlight
the horizon, prepare for the coming of the moon.
Perhaps from your celestial perch,
it was *you* who painted that sky
bluer-than-blue, a thank you for all
the good, now that the pain has died too.

31

II

"The singular morning glory that knows
precisely when to raise its head toward light."

~ Sandra Becker, "Now and Then,"
Dread Islands

Orphan Train
Lavinia Kumar

I. First Read This
Homes are wanted for the following children: BOYS: Ages, 10, 6, and 4 years; English parents, blondes. Very promising, 2 years old, blonde, fine looking, healthy, American; has had his foot straightened. Walks now O.K. Six year old, dark hair and yes, good looking. Part of an 1893 ad in a Tecumseh Nebraska newspaper.

II. 200,000, 1853-1929

The rail tracks, the long line
of carriages, the Orphan Train
(not one train)—up to 300 children
riding east to west like cattle,
Texas, Kansas, North Dakota, Nebraska,
farms where help was needed.

Children from Germany, Lebanon, Russia
(some not able to find parents
who'd come before),
herded on trains in New York,
dropped off across all the states.

Children trained in best behavior—
manners, poems, songs—
to show off,
entice new owners,
lined up small to tall
in front of the train
or in nearby church.

Children flung like woodchips,
or rough-hewn dice,
station by station,
year by year.

Cliff Swallows

Lynn Fanok

"a voice out of the past, not very loud, that went on
saying a few simple things to the solitude eternally."
~ Willa Cather, *The Song of the Lark*

His ominous bellow
resounds from a dark place.
He punches a fist
through our kitchen wall.

One Sunday morning
he squeezes and holds our mom,
gushes, "I love you."
I want to believe him—
that this is the way of love.

Years later in a rage,
he threatens her
with a kitchen knife.

I find a hole,
a cave, crawl in,
lie down, lose myself
among the swallows
that tumble over and over—
a smoother landscape.

Hungry Ghosts

Katherine Hahn Falk

Ghosts may not be mentioned around Lily.
She is emphatic about that. She does not want to know
about anything she can't see.

After my friend Laurie's mother died,
her Tibetan Buddhist brother-in-law, Kunga,
said he was cooking for her mother, so Laurie asked,

"Why? She's dead." "Ghosts get hungry too," he said.
Thankfully, every Buddhist Temple sets a place at the table
for the Hungry Ghost. Are there enough places

set for the number of ghosts? Do they share the offerings?
How much food and drink do ghosts want or need?
How do they use it? Where does it go? Do they drink tea?

I will cook for you if you go first. Day and night.
I will say the mantra three times, sit at the table with you
in case you're there during that Bardo stage,

in between the day you leave your body
and when you go to begin your next life 49 days later.
Buddhist monks know where a person's next life will be.

They told Laurie that her mother would be the middle boy
in a family of three sons. It's said people choose parents
by the lessons they each need to learn.

Once only, in a big silent voice, I issued an invitation,
"Calling all souls. If there is a soul out there
that needs a body, come on in" ………….. and Lily did.

Balanced Enough

~ for Lucas

Black-eyed Susans have had their yellow-
      visible-from-a-distance season. I lean
from my scooter, cut their sturdy stems,
      then you and I crumple their deep brown

cones, black seed raining. Diligent, you work
      a small rake to scatter the seeds. *There you go!*
you say, kneel, and pat them into the ground.
      You hunch down closer like someone about

to decode an unfamiliar language. I imagine
      that I join you kneeling in the earth, cool loam
dampening my jeans—what a cannonball of joy
      it would be to dig! The last blooms of Annabelle

hydrangea present their leaning heads like froth
      of large waves about to break. Red maple leaves
fling themselves against humming sky. You give
      chase across early-fall and catch a leaf that

for the first time in its life has let go. I let go too
      and stand, my left leg shaking with spasms
that you think mean dancing. Propped against
      the shed, I'm balanced enough to swing

your arms, dance in this falling shadow of a day.
      You hand me a loosened leaf. Oh!—to yield to wind
as this leaf, to mimic soaring clouds, birds, to step
      out of my doorway as having survived the earthquake.

You move on to collect stones, cicada husks, acorns.
      Red leaves—like you—chatter near the fence.

Tokyo Underground Prayer

Mary Jo LoBello Jerome

On the Hibiya line, I watch my daughter laugh
with two friends: fourteen, long-haired, short-skirted,
their American legs in the aisles.
They snort and bend and poke each other into fits,
oblivious of other riders. Their
perfect faces crease with joy. And the way
their eyes glint, are those tears? I try to recall
a time when laughing was the only thing that hurt.

The train rocks and screams, the passengers
lurch silently, they clench and clutch.
All eyes behold the girls: swaying and floating,
their voices rise like balloons, like clouds, like hallelujahs.
Women on the train squint sidelong at them,
unsure what reserve of poise they need to step over
or ignore that tangle of candy toenails,
and flip flops, and legs, legs, legs.

Sit up straight and shush, I want to warn.
Close your knees. But I know just what they'd say.
Those pert new chests straining their thin tee-shirts
seem a tacit rebuke. I roll my shoulder blades
back, hoping mindful posture will correct
what a good bra and calcium pills can't.
A gray-haired man in a suit sidles near.
He eyes these lives bubbling up before him,

just out of reach. His gaze swims on their bare skin.
I tense and my hard look says: *Don't you dare.*
The gully-lined scowl and hooded eyelids
of my weathered face should stop him dead.
Yet he moves nearer, cocks his head, and grabs
the pole behind their seats. He's close enough
to touch. He plants his feet and balances,
and I'm up, ready to charge, heart pounding.

Mary Jo LoBello Jerome

But he rests. Clasps his hands behind his back,
in reverie, reverse supplication,
and poised, closes his eyes and sniffs the air
over their heads as if pausing in a garden
to remember some sweeter time. The girls
laugh, unaware. I ease back, raise my head,
and catch a whiff of a wafting honeyed scent.
I inhale a hint of holy incense. Then I let go.

Even Today—Iowa

Phyllis Purscell

" ... even today honeysuckle means Dakota
and long summer evening*" Living on the Plains,*
~ William Stafford

Those occasional late summer evenings that glow a rich rose
mean Iowa and your father choosing the first watermelon
of the season with a practiced thump.

Children lived by counting down to the next holiday,
the brief time between Thanksgiving and Christmas,
then long, serious winter months, broken by the rare,
yearned for snow-day.

If you go back years later you will be careful
to avoid the new mall residents are so happy with.
You'll hunt out Bayliss Park, Lake Manawa and Benton Street.
Your old house.

You'll stand on the topmost bluff overlooking
the Missouri and remember when you'd never gotten
further west than Oglala, Nebraska.

A Visit to The Country

Lynn Fanok

We pull up to the faux red brick bungalow
with its front garden display of hens and chicks,
red poppies, velvety lambs ear, and plump bumble bees
perched on the heads of black-eyed Susans.

We help Dad unload our bags, enter the cramped
kitchen ruled by Bapcia's rolling pin.
Blueberry, apple, rhubarb pies—their crusts gleam
under our greedy fingers and mouths.

Yisty! Yisty! Eat! Eat!

Inside, we play hide the thimble.
Outside, I discover a box turtle,
adopt it for the weekend,
and force-feed it wild strawberries
as if only I know what's best for it.

We use the outhouse in a pinch,
fight over the solitary beat-up bike,
scout for hoof prints left by
the elusive *Jersey Devil*.

Grey sap crawls down the lofty pine.
Encircled around its trunk, a plywood table,
vinyl kitchen chairs underneath.
Relatives drink, boast, laugh, shout.

My father sits till dark. Legs crossed,
he takes a drag from his cigarette.

This is the closest he'll come
to his vanished country.

Driving to the Moon

Mary Richardson Miller

Restless for the road, I dream
of highways all over the universe.
Here on earth I'd drive anywhere,
anytime; it's not the distance, it's
the drug of it: speeding up the road
with the commerce of the country,
speeding past trucks hauling
horses, houses, and rust red cattle,
sunflowers, steel rods, and Perdue Chickens.
Roads connecting, dissecting, weaving
up and down the coast, out
across plains, mountains, highways
steaming, gas fuming, dust flying.
      I'd even drive to the moon
and back if there was a road.
I'd head for the highest peak, try
to touch the dome of the sky;
I'd see galaxies whirling, volcanoes
erupting, clouds moiling mayhem,
high winds sweeping stardust,
my heart singing as I hunt the heavens
yoo-hooing for God.
        No longer
imprisoned by my own planet
I'll consider mapping the way
to Mars amid the ordered chaos,
aim for the mastery of mystery,
in sync with the universe,
restless once more.

It Was a Time When
Cars Were Cars

Connie Wrzesniewski

And I loved that old car, brand new, right off
the showroom floor, a '72 Chevy Nova,
just waiting there, windshield staring at us,
her bumper smiling.

It was a time when cars were cars
with genuine metal bumpers that rarely folded
when hit. We called her Chitty-Chitty Bang-Bang.
Able to reach sixty in an instant, her V-8 engine
could declare lift off if only her roof sported
a rotary blade. She took us everywhere.

Later that trusty car battled wind
that ripped across the Jersey Parkway
knuckles whitened on the steering wheel
charging buffeting gales on the way to the shore.

And who could ever forget
when Beth, my daughter and I—
like Thelma and Louise—crashed through
the one-armed toll cop, bits and pieces of it
flying above us like confetti as we stormed across
the Ben Franklin Bridge?

About three years later, Beth stripped off her
hubcaps when we said our final goodbyes to
our faithful friend—she was a good steady car,
that Nova.

Off Pine Tree Road

Phyllis Purscell

It was one of your rare Sundays off,
a spring day. We started out on Orange Turnpike.
Besides the two of us, who else? The little girls,
of course. And one of your lost boys. Billy, I think.

The road circled the ashram and the lake.
We met the same woman twice, carrying
her various pickings. You said she seemed the sort
who goes home, takes out her old college botany
text and looks things up.

We'd have gone home, put on the kettle
and laid a fire. Atoms of the Sunday air resting
in our blood. Our breath still stirring on that road.

Solitaire

Connie Wrzesniewski

Rainy Days and Mondays,
~ The Carpenters

Mother taught me,
Aces go at the top,
below that, one card
face up, six face down.

The queen always goes
beneath the king,
black on red,
red on black.

Remember to alternate colors.

She'd slide an arm
around my shoulder,
lean in to point at the cards,
brush a soft cheek past

the crown of my head.
All the while, a patter
of raindrops on windowpanes
played in the background:

rhythmic relaxation,
tonic for a lazy afternoon
in ordinary harmony
at the dining room table.

Urban Remedies

Mary Richardson Miller

Housed high in glass
and steel I long for

earth, so I garden
in slow stages at heights

where hawks are at home.
Pot by pot I plant herbs,

a language learned from
my mother.

I, too, grow feathered dill
and rosemary redolent

of pine, pungent thyme
and strength found

in parsley—herbs her hands
knew well, digging deep

in the earth of her garden.
Up where hawks

fly, I repeat the dialect
of aromatics, seasonings,

linguistics of silver leaf,
fragrance of lavender, their

tendrils tender, glowing,
ready to cleanse, purify.

Counter

Bernadette McBride

"Nothing Can Be Where the Word Fails."
~ Stefan George (1868-1933)
~ for Steve Nolan

But what of the index finger to the lips?
The squeezed hand. The funeral hug.
Too, the substantial dream, the flight of image
across a silent screen, twirl of a leaf to loam.

Pilate's wife gives her visioned warning;
Scrooge spends the night in eidolon;
Hamlet urges Horatio: *believe you've seen*
the wordless visit. More

than vacant utterance is the mother
shushing her infant at midnight, the abandon
of lovers' beds, the sudden hitch of breath
at the expanse of sea at the feet.

Note to a friend who believes
herself mute

Susan H. Robbins

I know the stories you tell yourself.
I know how you moor yourself at the root
of an abandoned willow,

how you craft your heroines in words
hoping they nest among greying
of the fallen leaves upon which you sit.

What I ask of you is to remember
the hour when you once painted the sidewalk
that connected our front doors, the sidewalk

scarred by root and ice and roller skate.
Do you remember how I painted it
fire-engine-red as a backdrop for shades

of purple quotes you lifted from your diary—
the one you offered that one summer,
to the willow as an incantation, a war chant?

And do you remember the hour when
you named your cat, Miss Simone de Beauvoir,
and knew why?

What I ask of you, dear friend,
is to let go—just let go
and do it, out loud.

III

"Honor the stones that held you down
and covered you.
How else could you have known
this strength?"

Sandra Becker, "Rock Rose,"
At the Well of Flowers

Summer of the blue sarong

Susan H. Robbins

I had bought it by the sea—in a shop so overcome with fabric
that the metal hangers had no breadth
to dream.
Yet I had found it—ripe with
cornflower expressions within a sweeping swirl of indigo,
paisleys with tamed shark-like teeth—although I don't recall
paying as much mind to the pattern—as I did the candor
in the sapphire of the mid-evening blue.

Did I tell you I had bought it by the sea?
I did, didn't I?
On an easy street in Cape May—before
it recomposed itself into a shopping arcade—
complete with faux daffodils and cascading
water fountains garnished with counterfeit stone—
ashen, uneven, in profile.

What has it been? Twenty-two summers of wearing?
Twenty-five?
Has it really taken that long
to love how these bones fit the narrative
of that sarong?
Faded at the bodice. Soft. Threads strong.
Solo now. Bathed in the late afternoon
of a wood thrush song, grand boughs and garden greens—
so much green—limber with breeze.

First time that I can recall holding serene enough,   true enough,
wide enough,
to wear it properly
for the sea.

After "Only until this cigarette is ended"

Bernadette McBride

~ Edna St. Vincent Mallay
~ for Sandra

Or just before its ash grows long and falls
as gin-soaked forms, bent to one another, grieve
across the sawdust floor where closing hour stalls
the spell that held them, and they leave.
Or morning's light crawls through the empty street,
where alcoves welcome nightly rubble spent
are you're, once more, in dream still incomplete,
not the substance of embrace, or tuned words lent
then taken back, but shadow and a song recalled,
a welling in the core still not subdued,
our season long asleep but still enthralled
by shed youth's optimistic amplitude.
And you may, too, before you, evening sprawled,
yield to this persistent muse, be wooed.

A Pilgrim Dwells Here

Susan H. Robbins

I zip up my deep saffron
rain slicker over charcoal shirt

distressed at the seams,
as a mist emboldens little wings
of wanting.

April purrs faint breaths within
the woody pulp of March.

A dog slips its leash
sensing indigo skies.

I work a patch of earth,
long and narrow,
boasting a single dandelion,

blessing the earthworm,
cursing the stones, as I
move my thirsty hands
from the latch of a garden gate

to fill a slate-gray watering can
half-way
with fairy stories.

Her Continuing Metamorphosis
Katherine Hahn Falk

Sometimes she sits on the green shelf
among the flowered canisters of cotton,
toothbrushes, toothpaste and powder.
Sometimes she perches with the spices
and different colored peppers or
the poetry books of one whose words
she values and who refuses to be named.

She may do this from a yoga posture
and from the shelf watch her own body
do a shoulder stand or the cobra or the dog.
Some days she is a dog with a little Mohawk
tuft of hair, a dog comprised of five breeds,
and another day a parrot that will live
half a century and repeat its days out loud.

Sometimes she is the mother of a teenager
telling her to go away or she must supervise
a little bull full of bravado bursting out at meetings.
Sometimes she listens in the audience to poems
that arrive on bicycles or in limousines with white
kid-leather seats to whisk her away, champagne
and the promise of sweet lemongrass.

At the Kitchen Table

Monica Borrin Flint

The other morning, coming downstairs,
I sensed a tingling in the air—a freakish
early morning lightning streak, perhaps.
But then I caught the scent
of buttered toast and the sounds
of kitchen merriment.
I knew I had visitors.

I peered around the door jamb
and must confess to a jolt of surprise
at finding, around the kitchen table,
The Buddha, Jesus, Muhammad
Peace be Upon Him, and Moses.
Believe me, they were instantly recognizable.

I joined them, delaying only to grab
a jar of marmalade they might enjoy.
The conversation flowed freely,
eloquent, as you'd expect,
also full of fun: loads of jokes
all very silly, and giggling.

They loved the binoculars
taking turns to watch woodpeckers,
chickadees and squirrels at the feeders,
and gasping in delighted unison
when a fox hurried past among the trees.

And then, before I knew it, they were gone.
"But were they real?' you ask.
"Don't you think you were probably dreaming?'
Oh they were real. So real.
As real as the oracles.
As real as eggs is eggs!

And the Cheese Stands Alone

Bernadette McBride

~ an homage to fromage, by Gruyere

Does anyone know (or care)
what life's like for a chunk of Gruyere?
Sure, at times I hooked up to play
with a fine—I mean *fine* Chardonnay,
but eventually she was lured
by the scent of a smooth Camembert.

Let me tell you that in my youth
I made out with a sweet Vermouth
till she left for that rich Gorgonzola
who'd been wooing full-bodied Rioja
neither were good mates for him, though
—for each, he was too sharp a tooth.

I once wed Nouveau Beaujolais
first daughter of lovely Gamay,
and thought for a time I might like
to be dad to some new little tyke:
Baby Gouda, or Swiss? Mozzarella?
But that plan never did go my way.

And now, here, in the middle of life
I find I'm not into a wife.
Though I've enjoyed the good company
of Rieslings and one light Chablis,
my friends now are bright Asiago
and a Bleu—grown too mellow for strife.

I've learned, too, I'm delightfully prone
to living my life on my own—
oh, I engage in occasional flings
with Champagnes or other Sparklings.
But these days I'd rather befriend,
spend my time with an aged Provolone.

The Nature of Air

Seven twenty a.m., arriving at Terminal 3
on the monorail for my Virgin America flight:
misty expanse of San Francisco Bay beyond,
laid out like an architect's model.

Then, without ado, Leonardo da Vinci
appears beside me, traveling, it seems,
through time for the first time! His surprise
morphs almost at once to understanding,

to recognition and then joy, as he takes in first
the smooth, driverless train—
then the silver birds with outstretched
wings gliding to takeoff,

one elegantly following the other
rising as the leader disappears
into the haze of height, light, speed, and time.
As Leonardo registers the word *Virgin*

on planes' flanks, puzzlement
registers on his high brow,
only to dissolve into smiles
as he connects his *Virgin of the Rocks*,

and cartoons of *Virgin and Child*
to his *Codex on the Flight of Birds*,
his *Studies of Bats' Wings*
and on *The Mechanics of Landing Gear*.

"Will you join me on our flight east?" I invite him.
"Won't I just!" he says.

Full Moon on a November Night in the Woods of Hickory Run

Connie Wrzesniewski

Frost on the moon,
the night is silvered,
even the stars shiver,
wrapped in shawls of fog.
How eerie the mist.

A feathering of ice crystals
clings to shagbark leaves
that crunch as I plod
deeper into the stand
of once-friendly oaks.

The red fox chills my bones
with his raspy bark, crack
of branch splits the night
and a buck leaps across the path,
heightens my fright.

Snowy owl hoots
into the sleepless wind that rustles
through pines at the edge
of the wood. Topaz eyes pierce
the tarry shadows.

Grey wolf stands erect, framed
by soft sway of evergreen, inclines
his head toward the moon
and in scooping arcs, howls
into the chiaroscuro before him.

Birds in the Mist

Lavinia Kumar

I saw her in the bushes, her basket full.
Through mist I saw two men in a small boat
as they returned after night fishing,
a hundred birds flying around them
in the cloud-dark dawn.
As they reached shore they heard her giggle
and looked. But she hid
her face behind a lotus blossom.
And I was afret—she was too young.

As they stepped onto the bank, they whispered.
One walked toward our girl.
She stood, her smile inviting
as she let the lotus fall in her basket,
which he lifted, placed his hand over hers,
led her away slowly as if to a dance.

Ursula Comes into Her
Own & How

Wendy Fulton Steginsky

Ursula wanted to set his hair afire
& the grass & blood-orange hibiscus bush

& his punishing body, pinning me beneath
like an insect on a specimen board.

She watched from a distance as time spooled out
and bare cedar branches extended into the dark like horns.

In that grain of time, Ursula decided to ratchet up
her feisty quotient and sign up for aikido classes.

She practices self-defense all day long,
karate chopping the air everywhere we go.

The only problem is she sometimes jumps
the gun, sensing danger as imminent

when it really isn't. But where would I be
without Ursula, the warrior?

Dear Ursula, clad in leather and chains,
one foot cocked against a wall.

When One of Us Is No Longer   *Christine Caruso McKee*

The other night
I remember thinking
but not saying,
even as it was happening,
that these moments
when we are just sitting
around the kitchen table
having a cup of tea and conversation,
will someday hold an
extraordinarily
exquisite
beauty.

Twilight's Small Gestures

Wendy Fulton Steginsky

Leslie kicks her heels absently
against a concrete wall at dock's end,
peers overboard, loses herself in the play

of water—the darkening ruffles that slap
and smack the way young children tease
each other's boundaries, salt spray

plumes like clustered branches
of whistling pines bursting silvery-grey.
Sea's swell rolls over and over—

This, her favorite time of day—
comfort after daylight's harsh teeth,
when sun's a smoldering fire

on water's surface, clouds stack
in the sky like sea gulls' wings
and easterly wind becomes

squeezed breath through an oboe.
Fuzzy-edged light fades, belongs
neither to one world nor the other,

boats and bay grape trees begin
to lose their shape, darken, disappear—
everywhere, small, quiet gestures of dying.

Unafraid, Leslie appreciates embers
or dust turned to beauty for this brief hiatus—
before night's muscular song falls and rises.

Third-Quarter Moon

Marie Kane

~ for my friend, Sandy

This late November night announces itself
as Indian Summer—70° at eleven p.m.
The wind almost takes the front door
when I open it to view the massive oak

        across the street that flings itself crazy in windy
        warmth. Fall has turned its heel, pivoted back
        to summer. Yet winter's ice and snow—
        January's queen—will soon force branches

to the ground in homage to her. How pleased
she will be when they *snap*—something you
could not bear. I've convinced myself that's why
you left us in November—to not endure winter's

        madness, the loneliness of snow-covered,
        indifferent roads. Surprising frost glazed
        the ground earlier this fall, predicting, you said,
        winter's grim damage. What no one realized:

your certainty that no crocus nor snowdrop
slept beneath your landscape. No anticipation
of spring's melt since no flowers would climb
toward light to fold open purple and white.

        So I shouldn't be surprised that you guaranteed
        winter would not touch you. Later that evening,
        the third-quarter moon rose, its left side bright
        with reflected sunlight.

IV

"Something about being boundless. Something
about light that seems to say,
All will be well, there is so much more."

Sandra Becker, "Boundless,"
Imperfect Matter

Poem in October

Marylou Kelly Streznewski

Sometimes, I don't believe October.
Those trees up the hill could not have turned
such color overnight. I dreamed in color,
that is all. Tomorrow it will go away.
But the trees are worse, and I get drunk
on claret, burgundy, burnt umber and wine red.

The night comes quickly, closing in,
But oh the days when clouds climb
the sky and all the colors are two
beats brighter than red.

It's a gypsy month. I get restless and
a little crazy. I take long walks. I write
poems to the green-banked trees up the hill,
suddenly shot through with antique gold,
chrome yellow, the pasture turned sable brown,
like an animal's coat.

I sit on my stump in the sun. Someone
set fire to the woods up the hill. They are
lit all day with flickering sun-flames. There is
work to do but I sit on my stump.

I can cut grass when the fire is gone,
pull weeds when the yellow mums are dead.
Not now. Not now. I must attend October,
pay attention to the wind.

I buy apples now from a sun-warmed,
stone-cool barn heaped with scarlet and emerald.
Our cellar is perfumed with treasure,
the kitchen with apple pie.

I yank the gentian petunias from the ground.
They went wild and their beauty became a nuisance.
Piled in the garden cart tumbril, they rumble with
nodding purple heads like so many Frenchmen,
up the hill to the compost heap, their place of execution,
their fate better than ours. They will be food
for roses, not for worms.

I pull the gladiolas out and put the tulips in.
Delicate glads must be sheltered from the cold.
Tulips need a smack of winter, just like people.
Some do their best when cared for and coddled,
praised beyond belief. Others need a cold blast
of adversity to bloom in the bracing air of Spring.

I had a child in October, lost a child too.
Gave one life and bright blue sky, wrote
a song for the child-who-never-was,
so I would not forget and fill that space
within myself.

In the five-day space that ends the month,
October tells us to celebrate the birth
and mourn the child never born.
A raggedy V of geese calls from the evening sky.
I stand on foolish tiptoes, waving goodbye.

A Black Stone

Mary Jo LoBello Jerome

water worn with pleasing heft,
smooth, almost heart-shaped but lopsided,
the misshapen valentine we found
on that rocky Cape Breton coast, an oddity
so appealing that even Eros lost
in thought would have rolled it rhythmically
in his palm for long minutes before he
dropped it back into the sea. One lobe, distinctly
larger, and we joked half afraid on that misty
beach just three days after our wedding,
our bare feet raw in the surf, would this rock
be the mineral totem of our life?
Crooked, petrified, solitary.
Not us, we vowed. I snuck it home. And now
decades later, forgotten then found
again and again in the velvet-lined jewelry box
inherited from my mother, it's still solid, silky,
metamorphic, asymmetrical,
one lobe more hulky, forever beating
harder for the weaker side. The smaller
ventricle, sometimes me, sometimes you.

Wood and Bone

Lynn Fanok

A wooden icon of Mary
and child sits silent, sacred
on my fireplace mantel along
with small carved birds and
boxes, all gifts from Poland,
carved from linden trees.
One small box has a hidden lever
that springs open a secret drawer.
I like to think it holds this memory:

One Sunday morning,
lounging on the bed with my mother,
my father thumps his sternum.
We look on, listen to him boast
in his thick European accent,
Jesus Christ was a carpenter
like me.
I believe him.

Uncle Joe's Chili Sauce   *Marylou Kelly Streznewski*

Not what's Heinz-bottled on a supermarket
shelf, but Mason-jarred in memory.
I was a thirty-something relishing

the gift, homemade after many years
hiatus, telling my children to enjoy
the lumpy pickles, peppers and tomatoes,

one small taste of which had the power
to time travel me back to being eight,
tasting hotdogs at a family picnic
for the next uncle, cousin, going off
to "basic training," going off to war.

The sun, the grass, the charcoal grill, playing
kid games in my favorite red sundress
with no sense that the goodbye kisses they
teased us into giving our handsome cousin
could actually be real goodbyes.

I Can't Seem to Meditate Any Longer   *Steve Nolan*

I went to the mountains of Afghanistan
but never made it out of the foothills
of the Himalayas, never met a rishi,
let alone sat with one in meditation.

Samadhi? What do I know of samadhi?
I never learned to break down the wall
of "I am." My prayers built a bulwark
that said I am down here in the muck
while you sit majestically in heaven.

The problem of suffering in the world
frequently keeps me from joy—but then
I hear music, someone asks me to dance,
a dispensation that dares one to die
before death, prance on your own grave
before it is occupied.

                    Laugh, because
that is the one sound you can still believe
is an answer to your prayers.

Proximity

Christine Caruso McKee

~ for Pam and Herb

This morning, earth pushes east
and petals of light flit through leaves
onto the bedroom wall. The trill of birds
warms the air. Clatter of trash men,
news-traffic-weather! pours from the radio,
and *Gram, breakfast's ready*
booms up the staircase to wake me.

I love the timbre of plate on table,
spoon on saucer, tea kettle's sss-*scree*-sss.
As my eyes adjust, my knees bang
against themselves and the sheets, and my feet
flounder, seeking their balance with the world.
Fitting into slippers under the bed, I recall
that two pairs used to cuddle there together.

Alas, again, that secret part of my soul
wafts away and, like a child following the path
of a balloon across the sky, I feel it zeppelin
through the window in search of you.

And I remember long ago lying in the barn,
lulled by braying, soothed by bleating,
the stillness of dusk across the loft—
a gossamer cape once swirled, now finding rest—
the hint of tobacco, and you, whistling that nameless tune,
turning to me saying, *Forever.*

Mouth Painted* Card

Elizabeth Rivers

~ for Sandy

1.

We made a song
we couldn't sing,
You had your nerve,
I had mine, too.

You sent a note
addressed to me,
envelope stamped
"animal rights."

What's right for you?
What's right for me?

2.

You wrote good-bye—
mouth pain-ted card—
peonies so
flushed and fat

by Hseng-Lung Lo;
you improvised,
wrote her name twice,
your last refrain

I can't forget,
your last refrain.

3.
Mouth-pain-ted card—
red peonies
painted for you
painted for me—
I can't forget
your last refrain,

I can't forget
your last refrain.

*art made by using a brush held in the mouth

A Question

Phyllis Purscell

When all the promises you have made
to yourself and others have been kept

or broken, and you can acknowledge
that everything will either be all right

or it won't, and—furthermore—that
you are likely to die without knowing

which, then—if you are sufficiently
forgiving of yourself and others,

might there be something like a harvesting
of your life, a celebratory feasting on it?

Caravanserai

Sandra Becker

The heavy-lidded night
   will have its way with us again.
Who can we blame?
   Who can blame us?
The caravan of mind
   must lay down its load and rest,
reflect on the vast sky,
   puzzle over the moon's hieroglyphics,
mourn the ghosts' footsteps in the sand.
   Tomorrow, no doubt, will arise
from sleep, a camel
   with its stiff and awkward legs,
carry us to the next well,
   patch of grass, tree of manna.
The call of an invisible flute
   heard while we slept
will keep us plodding on.

Katherine Hahn Falk, Poet Laureate for Bucks County, Pennsylvania, in 2017, was selected by the Lehigh Valley Engaged Humanities Consortium for a program funded by the Andrew W. Mellon Foundation. Katherine studied poetry at the graduate level, has won poetry contests, and enjoys teaching poetry to students in their classrooms.

Lynn Fanok's poetry highlights her Ukrainian cultural heritage and memories of her father, a WWII labor camp survivor. Her poetry has appeared in *Painted Bride Quarterly* and several other journals. Her first collection of poems, *Bread and Fumes,* was published by Kelsay Books in 2021. Lynn organizes and leads a monthly poetry reading series at the Newtown Bookshop in Bucks County, PA.

Monica Borrin Flint was born in England, where her parents had found refuge a few years earlier after their original country, Poland, was brutally conquered, first by the Nazis and then by the Soviets. She moved with her family to the U.S. in 1989, where she eventually met Dr. Christopher Bursk, who inspired her to write.

Mary Jo LoBello Jerome is the 2019 Poet Laureate of Bucks County, PA. Her poetry and fiction have been published in *Stillwater Review, River Heron Review, Schuylkill Valley Journal, U.S. 1 Worksheets, Little Patuxent Review*, among others. A former teacher, she has freelanced for the *New York Times*, *Scholastic,* and other publications.

A three-time Pushcart Prize nominee and Bucks County Pennsylvania Poet Laureate, **Marie Kane** has published three collections of lyric and narrative poetry. Her last, *Persephone's Truth* (2018), includes art by her husband, Stephen Milner. Kane was diagnosed with multiple sclerosis in 1991; much of her work is informed by her experiences with this disease.

Lavinia Kumar is a poet, scientist, and artist. She has published two poetry collections; the latest is *The Celtic Fisherman's Wife: A Druid Life* (2017). She has written three chapbooks, the most recent being *Beauty. Salon. Art.* (Desert Willow Press, 2019). Her work has been published in the U.S., Ireland, and the U.K.

Bernadette McBride, author of four poetry collections, most recently, *Everything Counts* (Kelsay Books, 2019) is the poetry editor for the *Schuylkill Valley Journal*. Recipient of several honors, her poems have been published widely, both domestically as well as in the U.K., Canada, and at PRI's *The Writer's Almanac.* (bernadettemcbridepoetry.wordpress.com)

Christine Caruso McKee has loved poetry since early childhood; in 2002, she became more committed to writing poems. Her work has been published in *Bucks County Writer, Her Mark, U.S. 1 Worksheets, Schuylkill Valley Journal, Presence,* and others. Her book, *On Shady Lane* (Word Tech), was published in August 2015.

Mary Richardson Miller is a painter, photographer, and poet. She is the author and photographer of *The Women of Candelaria* (Pomegranate Artbooks) and has just completed her first book of poetry, *The Wild Returning.* She lives in Washington Crossing, Pennsylvania.

Steve Nolan was a therapist and career military officer in the U.S. Armed Forces. Upon his return from Afghanistan, his poetry was featured on National Public Radio in a story titled, "Mother, Son Share Experiences of War." He is the author of *Go Deep,* 2018, *and Base Camp,* 2020, both of Ragged Sky Press.

Phyllis Purscell spent her early writing years as a playwright, involved with The Women's Project in New York. Never having thought of herself as a poet, she somehow found herself writing verse. It was her good fortune to be directed to that amazing poet/teacher Christopher Bursk and his workshop.

Elizabeth Rivers enjoys bringing creative poetry writing to school children. She is the 2008 Montgomery County, PA Poet Laureate, chosen by Marie Howe, and the 2009 winner of the Robert Frasier

Open Poetry competition. She's published three books of poetry, the most recent being *Living in the Sky*, Kelsay Books, 2019.

Susan H. Robbins found her poetic voice during a moment of stillness after decades of wandering, for which she is profoundly grateful. Grateful, too, for the three awards received from the Philadelphia Writers' Conference and for the publication of her poetry in print/online journals. Robbins is the founder/host of a literary, music, and theater arts salon. (www.RhythmandVerseSalon.com).

Lynda Gene Rymond is the author of two children's books. She was a finalist for the 2018 Bucks County Main Street Voices Poetry Contest, and a runner-up for the 2019 Bucks County Poet Laureate contest. She lives in Applebachsville, PA, with her husband, painter Charles Browning.

Wendy Fulton Steginsky is the author of three books of poetry. She has been published widely in the Caribbean and the U.S. She was a runner-up for the 2017 Bucks County, Pennsylvania Poet Laureate contest. Her book, *Let This Be Enough* (Kelsay Books) was awarded Honorable Mention in Bermuda's 2018 Literary Awards.

Marylou Kelly Streznewski is an eclectic writer of poetry, fiction, and non-fiction, which have appeared in national publications. She has published three poetry chapbooks, *Rag Time, Women Words, Dying with Robert Mitchum.* and a full-length book, *Sitting in the Shade of My Own Tree* (Kelsay Books, 2020). Her two non-fiction books are *Gifted Grownups* and *Heart Rending-Heart Mending.*

Connie Wrzesniewski writes for the Bucks County Herald. Her work is widely published. She won third prize in Delaware Valley College Writers' Conference in 2014 and in 2015 was second runner-up in Bucks County Main Street Voices Poetry Contest. Recently nominated for a Pushcart Prize, she has published two chapbooks.

~ Sandra Lynn Becker (1954-2018) ~

Photograph by Stephen Millner

Sandra Lynn Becker grew up in Long Beach, New York. After earning a degree from CUNY Queens College, and a masters from St John's University, she later studied poetry with Martha Rhodes, director of The Frost Place in New Hampshire. In an interview with Lynn Fanok, the coordinator of the poetry reading series at the Newtown (P.A.) Bookshop, she explains, "Thus began a more serious study of poetry, not just as a survival tool, but as an artist." She adds, "My poetry became a portal to inhabiting my feelings and experience rather than trying to transcend it all."

Her poems have appeared in a variety of journals including *Comstock Review, Concrete Wolf, Schuylkill Valley Journal, U.S. 1 Worksheets, Main Street Rag, Wordgathering, Barefoot Review, Flesh & Bone,* and *Red Booth Review.* In 2012, her poem, "Sanctification of the Ordinary," was selected to be part of the James A. Michener Art Museum's (Doylestown, PA) collaborative art and poetry exhibition. On September 27, 2014, her poem, "A City Girl Feeds Country Cows," was read by Garrison Keillor on Writer's Almanac.

Becker relished her role as the 2014 Bucks County, Pennsylvania Poet Laureate, judged by Kim Addonizio and Kasey Jueds.

Sandy Becker published five books of poetry: *What Now, What Next: Other Ways to Pray* by Kelsay Books in 2018, *Dread Islands,* by Kelsay Books in 2015, *Imperfect Matter* by WordTech in 2013, *At the Well of Flowers* by Virtual Artists' Collective in 2011, and *Foreign Bodies,* winner of the Carolina Wren Press Chapbook contest in 2003. Joseph Donahue, final judge of the 2003 Poetry Chapbook Contest, said of Ms. Becker's work: "Like Emily Dickinson, or more recently, Paul Celan, Sandra Becker is a poet of ultimate moments rendered with spare, exacting strokes. These poems bring to difficult matters a spiritually attuned music that finds, in the ironies of illness, a luminous compassion."

Reading Sandy Becker's poetry will confirm Joseph Donahue's high praise.

www.ingramcontent.com/pod-product-compliance
Lightning Source LLC
Chambersburg PA
CBHW020949090426
42736CB00010B/1343